Lasso the Breath

Kristin Martin

Lasso the Breath

Kristin Martin

ISBN 13: 978-1-955338-20-2

Cover background, Canva, design by Lori Graham
Illustrations by Casey Davenport
Printed in the United States of America

POCAHONTAS PRESS

Check , VA
pocahontaspress.com

*This book is lovingly dedicated to my Mama,
Linda Louise, and her ever-faithful heart.
And to the beautiful Robyn,
who taught me how to sing again.*

K.M.

Table of Contents

Lasso the Breath

Kristin Martin

For Reckoners

I wanna crack you open
and pour you out like an inkwell
dip my old fashion feather pen
in the pool you make
and spread your soul across
a million blank pages
the ink's shades an electric neon
that glows in the dark and
occasionally pops up off the page

I wanna scrunch your body small
and sit you on the tip of a needlepoint
poke thread through the stars
and weave you into
a shapeless constellation
that makes unborn sailors sigh
on the planks of shadowed ships

I wanna take a swim through
the blackness of your eye's pupil
glide through the darkness
until my arms go numb
and when I'm done I'll rest
on the edge of your iris
until midnight comes
and the clock never changes

I wanna make you expand
along with the universe
until your pores are stretched so wide
they swallow up galaxies
creating pathways of recycled time
until you yourself
time itself
lasts forever

Orator

needs a campfire
        of encircled friends

to tell tales
to pass along

through her body language
and the gentle swaying
        of her heavy hips

as her arms cut languidly
through the night air
        hovering without sound

the air is fragrant
with the scent of spices
        and crisping wood

her audience becomes
entranced by the hypnotic
        humming of her voice

their hearts send
warmth out to the stars
        so that they will burn

a little longer...

Twilit Recognition

regarding yourself
with suspicion
                        across a distance

nighttime wide eyes
scanning the black horizon
for signs of your shadow-self

uncertainty curls the air
like a hot iron
and your lungs forget how breathe

                    (momentarily)

until the apparition
suddenly folds itself inwards
and disappears into

                    the crepuscular air

Your head
(for Robyn)

must be able to tilt/
        tilting of the mind,

    an ability to pause

REWIND

    clunking thoughts

side to side

      like a metal ball
in a pinball machine

   watching new facets

        GLOW

pathways interconnecting,

     and sometimes leaping

across

     TURN   IT   OVER

many more times ...

    making time to
  make sure

it sat UPRIGHT,

   (the prize is in the box
    you buried long ago

 in the

     backyard)

Bloodied Ideas

there's a creative impulse
surging within me
like the
banging expansion
of the universe

(I can't seem
to control it,
just like in
Neil Gaiman's
Sandman story...)

I dig my
fingertips into
brick walls
and drag them across
to spell these
bloody words
for lack of pen and paper

or a canvas, needle and
thread,
the dread of being

unable to focus
on an anyone else's
conception of reality

in danger of losing
my entire identity
to my imagination

(psyche run rampant)

it's unacceptable
to buy a house
on this street

what would people say
if I had no neighbors
to trouble myself about,
or what they might think?

wells of rainbow ink
splash out of
my waving arms
as I twirl in
circles within
an empty white room

the entirety

of its construction
functions as

my globular canvas

I lay at the
planet's core,
wrapped up
inside its
craggy terrain

like a kid tucked in
by their
favorite blanket

Floating in the Moonlight

my body holding steady

       at the top of the lake

I gather my senses here and to a point

I'm suspended in the dark-scape

        after image of day

still breathing, only this time at half speed

         untethered and gently bobbing

would you come up from under me

and devour my being?

        (my darling alligator man)

as you try to feel the sensations

of swallowing me,

how long will it take you to realize

neither of us was ever

where we thought we were

        to begin with?

soaking away displeasures

       in waters lacking any salt....

I slurp up each tear

hidden in the nooks of my eyes

        and stay hydrated until dawn

When the Devil Beckons

... I listen

sweet whispers,

a siren song,

just over those sloping hills

I hear his call

echoing over

darkened pastures

sent rippling

out the throat,

curving in midair,

circumventing flashes of faith ...

your words become

an index finger

bending inwards, beseeching,

"come here so I can pet you ..."

I'm a folded over vixen

and I do

what you tell me to ...

          infect me with your

noxious love,

drive my reasoning

        ever backward

into a sulphuric cave,

imprison my ego ...

       devoutly, I bend my knees

        and open my mouth,

--WIDE--

do I tremble in your

       heavy-scented atmosphere?

do the murky mustard clouds

        surrounding my head

serve as a bed

      for us to tumble into?

how so, transparent desire?

        cuffing my wrists

to the bedpost

made up, not of wood,

but of your outstretched,

jagged teeth...

stunned and poisoned,

I'm delivered into

your salivating lips ...

your tummy grumbles,

amply digesting our tryst

Hijacked

sometimes a memory
jumps you
1ike a thief in the night

how could you possibly
see it moving so quick
before it gets you?

you don't stand a chance
so don't kid
yourself, kiddo

you're gone before you go,
falling in a
flailing fashion

down through a
recently appeared
old-fashioned trap door

a memory wears
a cloak, carries
a sword, and rides
an ebony steed at night

it kidnaps you before
it kills you,
carrying you on its hump

you're along for a ride
through a fiery desert,
and it may take many days

"where to?" you beg,
but there's never going
to be a reply

the element of surprise
will get you
every single time

A Provocative Opera
(our chemistry is a conundrum)
2012

My lover
lets me lie there
my lover
is only as generous as me
my lover
asks me to climb the wall
so he can get a
better view of my
supple ass
my lover
thinks it's an apple
he can bite into

I'm a small girl
with a woman's
ample curves
to my lover
I'm everlasting candy
like a gobstopper
I satisfy his
sweet tooth
by convincing him
he's consuming me

Our bodies'
friction sparks
everything happens
on impulse
I wish I could say
I move like I do
on purpose every time
because now
he's begun looping
me inside him

       He whispers,
       "Eve ..."

       "Eve, my nymph,
       rose-lipped,
       tempt me..."

I obey
as his request
filters through
my skin and begins
a quick
set of twitches
while he
reads me like I'm morse code
-stitched-

My body is an anxious
ship lost at sea
but there he is
again
rescuing me
(not everyone in a
shipwreck is saved
he picks
me out special)
and I blush green
like a seasick
bride

He tries ordering
me at
fast food drive
thrus
(this confuses
everyone
besides
me)

I am
ever eager
to harness some
ancient power
and bestow life into
the mirage
he's seeing
(we both know that
I can)

He, so determined
of a certain
trajectory
and latently
forgetting
the monkey wrench
I hid in the sheets
while he was
sleeping

I'm not sure
he's aware of how good
I am at
sneaking about
making changes
to the bedroom
just for the fun
of watching his eyes
as they
unknowingly readjust

He's always asking
why I'm smiling
to myself

or laughing when
nothing's funny
little does he know
I've created two
worlds for us
-juxtaposed-
to keep this tryst
interesting

the electric
blue of my eyes
scans like xrays
across our minglings,

"That silly girl,"
he's thinking,

"always amused by
some such
thing..."

I know he'd ask
me to
let him in on it
if for a minute
he believed
I'm seeing things
that are
really there
(for indeed they
are)

He likes his women
a little delusional
(it secures his
sense of manhood)
I'm the doe
he hunted in the woods
for days and days
at last ensnared
but now he's got to
figure out how
to keep me

Men want a woman
who knows
how to
relax herself/
an inward
coax

I push him onto
his stomach
and lick behind
his ears
my naked breasts
brushing his shoulders

16

it's time to make
him shudder
my lover
perplexed and vulnerable
feels crushed
and loves it

He has
one thousand
switches in his
head
I flip on
and then off
one at a time
and then
all at once

I melt over him
gooey as caramel
pools of innuendo
drip off of me
like fine silk
across bare skin
he wants to
pull me over his head
and wear me like
a top

He chooses when
to trade places
yesterday he moved
our bed
next to the window
so he could watch me
climb in and out
of it naked
and blushing

(I'm not sure which
of those
pleases him more
but
blushing reflects honesty
and he likes his
women honest)

Our passion fits
my hips
like my favorite
casual blue jeans
(I never noticed
they had a back pocket
before his hand
went into it)

(I never noticed
the zipper barely

measured an inch long
until he was
pulling it down)
(such a mockery/
faux chastity, surely
that zipper
has betrayed
me)

I wonder
how it's possible
he never tires
of pursuing
me...
am I really
so delicious?
sugary as a pastry?
me?

I squeal when you
flip me
upside down
I find redemption
in your
purebred strength

these hours are
bandits
on the run
escaping unnoticed
but when
did the clock
take over
the kingdom?

I told him once
before that
rules are made
of ice
and I've flung
open the curtains
to let
the sunshine in

Cosmic battle with you
2013

I'll salt his
raw temper
and squeeze limes
in his eyes
so he can no longer
terrify

while he's distracted
with all that...

I'll be meandering
through
our household,
picking up each and
every piece of
every single
eggshell

I so dutifully
tried to scatter
across the floors...

alas, and
unfortuitously,
I attempted
nothing of this sort
for far too long

and so, the laws of time
have become
frozen and suspended,

and me?
I'm locked in his
blackhole prison

balanced just
at the edge
of the airless
event horizon
where I'll tumble
forwards

ever so slowly
towards infinity...

(I'm a
fixed point,
imprisoned for
the evil
I've wrought
in my life)

and although my
karmic prospects
are grim

I'll hover
along this rim
with no desire
for redemption...

And these Roots

ready pythons come to twist my neck

blackened soggy damp

         strong and tensile

drawn across my beak

     slowly slipping away

        and forgetting how to speak

pulled under and down

      (death's twisted embrace/

       vacancy of love)

ignescent specks now vanishing

      like chords of music, already played

       echoing in lower tones

     away away...

my essence crumbles

in the eye of a fading atom

     and the ground devours me

       to violent sleep

Eyes wide shut
2014

would I want my
eyes to be shut
at the time

       when I die?

I think I should
keep my eyes
open more often
to see through
the windows of the car
when we drive places
in resentful silence

       at nighttime hours

your twisting
of the wheel agitated
the harp strings
in my lungs and
I couldn't remember
the chord that the angels

       assigned my soul

how could I
have been seeing
with my eyes

       so gummed shut?

in time the
encircled ring
of an echo
will etch itself
across the timid sky
in the backdrop of a
purple and orange

       setting sun

I see it through
the crystal clear
waters of the infinite
only sheer curiosity
could carry me
all the way to here

       (and save my life)

Flashbacks and forwards

the mind
allows us fluidity of movement through time
(for we are otherwise prisoners
of this stringent dimension)

a fabric is woven
with a needle that is lodged
inside the eye of the mind

we tap dance across
this lump-ridden landscape
tripping over curbs and dips

send ourselves out upon on a unicycle
wheeling forwards and backwards
along haphazardly scattered
patches of thought

        << littered indecision >>

        << enumerated incomprehension >>

        << inability to credibly focus >>

truth is either lost
or grabbed back from the throat
of the forgotten

tickle the brain's nervelines
ride shaky trains
rusted and directionless
to nowhere destinations

which is as
perplexing as
drowning in quick sand
and
slumping down down

to the thresholds of seven hells

would you go again?
how often do you ride such decrepit lines?

how much courage can still be found in your heart?
how many tickets have you bought?

do you live to breathe your own answers?

or do you exhale happy falsehoods
with painted hoods
and duck beneath your pride?

<< insufferable lack of honor >>

<< asphixiated by toxic truths >>

<< regurgitating unproven wisdom >>

dissatisfied and
seated within
discordant rhythms
bleeding out prayers

screaming at God
for the melodies/(maladies)
she ascribed your life

bury the head of your indiginity in the sand
stand there like an idiot bird
believing no one can see you

stiff and stupid
lapping up lies
in the pools made by the gaps in time
then sucked backed down
from your mind's own version
of reality's timeline

Hovering way up dream

The hovering dream...

It's like my mind is rising above.

Or trying to physically raise itself above the
problems of my surroundings.

I am aching to launch over them and hover in midair
to safety.

I know that I know how to do this in the dream.

Like I've done it before and just forgot I was able to.

I can hover great distances based on my concentration.

Relocating my body away from all danger.

I can see the scope of things, a bird's eye view, my own
unique map of the world below me at large.

Perspective gives me wings, deep thought makes them strong.

I fly wherever I please.

Chainless, and with the ease of restful breath.

I often wonder how long my ability will last.

When I'll be forced to drop down again and forget.

I know that the dream will end.

And that when I wake up, I'll still know that I have a
secret...that I'm able to lift myself up high at will.

All I want is to share it with the people I love, and
to sustain my belief.

Help them to realize they can explore,
above it all, in giant swoops beyond grief

A Date with Freud

adroitly he interrupts

    the ticking clock

     of the second hand

     and the millisecond hand

  of the clock

      in my mind

    stops it

        willfully uncranks it

       taller than me he dangles it

  out of reach

     and this

    pisses me right off

     the crux of faux love

        denial

   a wall of

Succubus Doe
2013

men are surrounding me like vultures
I am crusty meat plastered on the ground

there's no amount of patience they have
(once I, their dinner, am spotted)

I'm driven into so many different beds...

so many ugly settings
  so many awkward situations
    so many unenjoyable scenarios
      so many dangerous encounters

       I am a huge seductress liar
       I loom over you with heavy wings

       I hope you don't mind if I park my car
       in your head for a while

I do not comprehend why it is
I feel the urge to flee into the arms of men...

subpar men
   inadequate
       unattractive
     unfunny
    old
   young
  mean
rude
   lewd
     unhealthy
       disgusting
       dirty
         smelly
      uncreative
    boring:

  M.E.N.

       I pray to the goddess
       to drain the nectar
       of her flower
       deep into my eyes
       so that I may wake up

          ARISE

but

I am a small young girl
    curled up in your sheets...

I am naked

        as I wait impatiently,
                        unstill,

        for your hands
        to run along my body

sometimes you get sidetracked
gabbing about this or that, and it makes me
want to

                TEAR YOUR TONGUE OUT

when you are touching me
waves of goosebumps roll along

                        underneath my skin,

                I feel it in ripples...

your touch turns me into a pool
  something's been dropped into,

        the ripples ringing outward,

                stretching bigger
                as they fade away...

I never told these men how I really think,
I led them to believe it was he
and only him

                (how very cruel I've been,
                such a naughty little vixen)

what's the matter?

I thought that's the way
you said you wanted me...

                said you wanted me...
                said you wanted me...

there's a vacancy titanic deep in my eyes,
only you've perched above the water
like a seagull

and the water obstructs your view...

you ask me to exist as a flame for you

you ask me at midnight to come over
  and bring some matches

when I get there in high heels,
you swallow up my waist

            with those huge arms
            pulling me to you

kiss me again and again and again
faintly, I hear you're
                        whispering

something
        as you ravage me...

            your rarely patient fingers already
            unbuttoning every inch
            of my body

(this is the part where I find out
who you really are, mister,

what you're all about anyway,

            and peak under that top hat
            you've been wearing
            this whole time)

I'll keep venturing forth into no-man's land,
lost in the seas of undying loves

            and deserts of desire...

the temperature right now is only slightly
above bone-chilling

            he warms my heart, he warms my soul

            he's a carpenter and he hammers out my dents

I'll wrap my legs around his ears
 and dangle my toes behind his head
   all the while laughing and loving him

                as he hoists me high...

(hopefully I've gone after a strong
one this time)

Ruins

it doesn't matter

how lost you are...

      in one moment

      or in one of those
      laden moments that lasts
      for a lifetime

      you will always come back
      to yourself

walking on my hands
in a

      GRAND STAND

enduring the deepening frowns that
flow down/
the huge bags of hollowed spaces
in my heart

these are the empty caves in which
my mind's eye

      shrinks down praying to
      see what it explores

a speck of hope
    shifts soundlessly
    among the messy crumbs

    of dirt on the floor

      (I'm slowly realizing I can hold out hope
      forever, as long as I
      carry this tune)

refusal to unknow the things
      that I know to be true

      I'm an ashy pile making up

my own ruins

Confessions from Outpatient Rehab
(2012)

There, this'll have to do. My stomach is a pit afire.
My head is cloudy.

I need to take better care of myself. I'm very tired.
When I get home I'll go straight up to nap.

Too much all at once. Sensory overload. I have to remember
that the people here love me.

I don't feel much like talking today. I hope the day here
is an easy one. I need to have faith they'll take care of me.

My tummy is in knots.

I wish I were stranded in the middle of deep woods. I wish
it was midnight and I was staring up at billions of clear,
sparkling stars as they light my way. Letting them blind me
with their twinkling.

I just want to be left alone to go to sleep.

Miles to go before I sleep.

I creep in search of doorways left unattended, cracked.
I'm well aware that I'm wide out in the open where people
can see me. I'm not trying to hide what I'm doing per se.

All I want is to be allowed to collapse for a bit. Or to
hibernate like a bear through the winter months of my emotions.

Allowing waves and clusters of life to fester, settle, breathe,
all the while granting me deep sleep.

I hope I'll be okay for groups today. I don't feel like myself.
Am I really even here?

Couldn't I just think my way out of materially being here?
Seems like I should be able to.

Life has been tinted poorly lately, like when I was overdosing
on mushroooms and reality turned to nightmare. The tinge is rust,
mold, all things drear.

My stomach churns and flips, tries regurgitating this scenery.
Everything's easy to throw up nowadays. I could so easily give
it all up. So easily at that.

(Too bad I know there'd be no point in that. Too bad I know better.)

I'm feeling anti-social as all hell. Why did I take that medication
this morning? Why am I such an idiot?

Why can't I go through the motions of life blindly, painlessly, disconnectedly? Why this hurt? This ache?

When does the ache fade? Is it stronger than me? Can I build a fortress that's stronger?

I hope I am able to function here today. I hope I didn't screw myself over.

I am a lost girl who needs help. But I'm weak, feeling pathetic, and cannot fend for myself. I need someone to recognize that I'm in pain, take me by the hand, reach out and cradle me.

Breathe deeply. Don't get ahead of yourself. This outpatient place is here to love and support you, to take care of you. Tell them you need help. Take your time, and let them in.

My heart feels so very heavy indeed.

There's a song by Avey Tare that talks about the sky:
"Too bad they can't tell me what is the right way."

A White Plane

cascades all the way

across neverwhere...

I'll see you there

in the blinking of one eye

I see my thoughts receding

ever backwards

tiptoeing among shards of

heavy glass

the sun reflecting off of each piece

blinding the other eye

pried open and vigilant

praying to rescue my decadence

out of the jaws

of the infinite

an insipid smile

conquering the faces

of the merciful

swords sharpened and raised

to my throat and my breast

I dare not dive into

the creamy pools

      of bitter forgiveness

and henceforth deliver

         my tired arms

       from their milk-treading

supplications

Ravenous Twinge

Mother's Day 2012:

Sober so difficult,
                          under the influence of

NO - things,

                    impossible.

Because I need something to distract,
worry, overtake my thinking, so I can
forget the perpetual

          down
                    in
                          the
                                    dumps.

Ceaselessly feeling

                    so low,
                              a solo,

rooted in solitude.

Pop caffeine pills,
                    drink black coffee.

Give me a drowsiness inducing antihistamine,

add the dramamine,
                          which keeps fading away...

I'm not kidding, ANY drug, with ANY effect
will do.

                    Will suit me up,
                              adequate-style.

Without the effects of the "any" drug,

                                    how am I supposed

to happily enough
                  represent myself

                              to all of them?

They and their
                naivete -

        - my envy,

                      my only
tattoo,

                      inked on the
tip of my tongue where
I can taste it.

                    "As long as she's not
                            drinking, she's okay."

       - - NO! - -

          Addiction's a nightmare
      you NEVER wake up from.

Don't trust me with

                      any drug
that produces

                      any effect.

I need the twinge.

It doesn't have to
be elaborate,

                      doesn't take much,
it's all about an "any"

                      twinge.

(I'm a cheap date.)

But drugs have betrayed me
                                        Caesar/Brutus style.

(Brutal is my vulnerability.)

                                        The tip of my tongue

flicks

                            my top row
teeth,

            scraping away
at the tattoo,

                        (my sister said it
                            was a mistake to
                            get one there, but did I listen?)

Any twinge at all will do.

Any anything that alters my perception.

            The experience I'm having
must differ from yours,
                                        or I don't feel OK.

Anxious, faux-meshing

                                        with you,
with all of you,

                                        CANNOT.

A pharmacy would help,
get me there

                                before the gathering,
the graduation, the big dinner,

the birthday celebration.

Who needs coke with
so much abundant,

over-the-counter
isopropyl?

Puff puff pass me right
along an
invisible, "any" mood changer

QUI CK.

How long I can
stand you all
depends solely
on the potency of my
twinge today.

(I warned you not to
project yourselves onto
me.)

I told you that if you're
not careful,
if I'm dry and desperate,
I'll settle for
YOU.

I'll suck you in through
my teeth cracks,
hold the hit long,
abuse the toke,
(YOU comprised).

I told you about the

                       sacred cows

      I once owned,

                   and butchered them,

(after holding out as

               long as I could.)

(I then proceeded to graze in

            their grassy

                         fields.)

"Sit still,

         fix your posture."

"Drink more milk,

           does a body good."

        I wander, lost at dusk, deep in
        a forest,

           overgrown and

   chaotic.

Any chance at chaos

         jumped into

     with zeal and

            undying gratitude.

Go ahead,

         judge me YOU PRUDE.

Guilty

Divine inner workings of the mind,
sublime relaxation of thought.

Intermingling coagulation, spunk.
Distraught, sickly coloration.

Put on the spot.
Distracted, uninterred.

Craving heaven, thrown in prison.

Confined spaces forcing responses
through cracks in the cement wall.

Hearing voices that aren't there,
but knowing I'm not insane.

Standing in front of a mirror,
running fingers through my hair.

Staring at my gaping mouth,
stuffing words back down my throat.

Swallowing in thick gulps,
choking on your misunderstanding.

Nightly endeavors through the forest,
searching for a long lost soul.

Like an unattached shadow that needs
to be sewn back on.

Threaded by fate, (accomplice of
life).

But I'm not listening, the tunes are
deafening.

I'm poisoning all the apples, and
reattaching them to the trees,
(whose eyes are leaves).

And with all those witnesses, how
could I ever escape uncondemned?

The jury is here, and I'm amongst them.

Finger-like branches wagging their
accusations at my face.

Disgrace. Disgrace.
Unloved heart, unchaste.

Fall into the deep dark pit.
Vanish without a trace.

Blackened Ocean

crashing...

the love of powerful things
and wading out...

then farther out...

watch as the next
navy blue curtain rolls in
tiny tornados swirling
at your toes

off balance and momentarily
froze
your body slurps
below the surface

your ears are drowning
in muted noise

while vicious hurricanes
blow over
your bent back head

and just then
you ask yourself:
does this wave
intend to let me up?

unearthly calm floats
like tiny bubbles
through your veins

as you smile through the water
that's sliding
through your teeth

before you can surface
time has stopped
your body silently suspended

eyes shut to black
for the purpose of "fun"

Hubble's Rubble

intelligent earthly
 creatures

(we beings)

sailing on horizons
 of veiled hypnoses

(no one can see
 beyond the light

we thought about
  twice)

but I find myself
 trusting

the sound
  of your voice

and letting you
 man the oar

sepia-toned rooms.
 become tinted

  in new colors

by ant-sized
 paintbrushes

  who wield
 themselves

you study the
 hooked shape

 of my hips
  in so much awe

 I would swear
 you'd seen

  the curvature
of the earth

 from space

for the first time

I've become a

      miniature astronaut
  cabled to the

     heart
        inside your body

so that I can
  provide my lungs

     with just enough

       oxygen

Owen's song
(Torchwood, 2013)

I'm so nervous
   to be alive I feel like
      I get to die
         over & over again
           every single day

   before I die
      I lie to your faces
         the lies, too, feel
           like death,
                 every time...

  So I cry for
    these things, I'm difficult
     to be around
            I'm told

    I'd apologize
      if you'd face me and listen
        to every last word
            of a tortured soul

My eyes are blank,
   you'll derive nothing
     from them

      (death has no one left
          to betray)

   Everything looks
      exactly the same,
        each tone a
          languishing
             death knell

     I dissolve into
       my surroundings
         like mist

     I'm compacted into
      a box world/
       rubik's cube
           nightmare realm

My eyes are fixed to see,
   trained to infiltrate,
     but ne'er
         participate

   Only one question
     is left mattering to

my tired mind...

When all this is over,
        will I still be so alone?

Musical Thread

I can hear the wind
blowing every night
it composes music
for an audience
of one

my ears dwell in
resting spaces
harmonies like beds
with staff-sized
blankets to wrap
myself up in

cocoon-like spinning
clouds of drifty thought
unfocusing the
learned logics
that reign as lords
of the meaningless

the winds comfort
the throbbings
leeched to my being
out for the very blood
I trust to keep me alive

let it go and fade
into the wind
it whispers low
like a subconsciously
implanted mantra

all ill intentions
are traced backwards
to mindless acceptance
in a labyrinth
of misdirection

and the seeming
death of choice

Suction - cupped
2010

she drags herself
through viny thickets
of indecision
across endless
thorn adversaries
scattering themselves
among the unmarked
terrain that she
is destined to breach
unknowing whether
this journey's end
will possess fruit
and meaning
or end in bleakest
swampy despair
no charity from
a heaven or a god
no hope except
the faint light
dying out in a
drizzle of lonely
clustered drops
from the murderous
raincloud overhead
but the forecast
never changes
this is her tragedy
and her limbs
are so tired
their strength
climaxed long ago
still she presses
forward and ever onward
regardless of the
failing heart
trapped inside her
decaying ribcage

when she arrives
at sunset
will there be anyone
waiting
to meet her?

not knowing
(solely hoping)
her muscles
unfailingly muster
the strength
to cross this
suction-cupped
ground

Black Cave Night Terror
Spring 2012

          trapped in a chamber
          filled with people
from my past

          only they're wearing
          different faces to
confuse me

          I can see from
          their rotted grins
          the pleasure they're
taking in my confusion

the decayed apple core

          of fear

my heart has become

          in this

purgatorial cavern of

          lost souls

trapped by me
          in this

          dystopian dream
          I've been having

          endlessing professing
          to be my friends
these zombies

          point me in circles
          and assure me
it's the way out

of this hopeless cave

          they call home...

only it's more

like an internment camp

or an underground

trailer park

w/ sulfurous stalactites
dripping mineral water
onto each of their
craggy noses

a distracting
and ever-present

echoing of noise

meant to flick
my pulse into flux
so I'll end up stuck

and wake up
forever interwoven
in a dance that was
shut down by fate

(there's no mother
waking me up for school
in the morning anymore)

I try nevertheless

to remember that

amidst the turmoil

of the twisted

dirty canals and

claustrophobic pathways

that I have not been
sentenced to
everlasting confinement
here...

I am no immortal
and upon this
hearty realization

I wake up

with fully illumined
blue eyes...

(sharp as shined-up knives)

Near my throat

I met a man
with magic in his hands...

they pressed into my skin
with such force

>   such pressure
>   right where
>   in every
>   corner
>   tension lurked

I didn't dare turn,
even to see his face...

all it was

>   was me
>   and his man-handling
>   hands

manhandle me some more...

I didn't need to beg, because
my pulse told him

>   about my crevices
>   the tension-filled
>   corridors
>
>   between
>   my shoulder blades

up & down

>   my
>   wound up
>   spine

vertabrae stiff

>   as nails
>   & bones

his thorough &

>   tough
>   pressing
>   pushed straight
>   through

all of the silly

brick barriers
I'd painstakingly
laid down

no need for an entire
army

    when all that's
    needed is
    one single pair

    of a knowing man's
    hands

man-handling

    my anxious
    tight body
    stress free & at ease

frollicking

    in a gentle
    green breeze

    (that only I
    can see)

Dreaming with Poe

strange, waking up
to this show that's on
post-deepest nap

and these dreams
revolving themselves
around the man
and the works of:

Edgar Allen Poe

my dreams,
their fragments,
already so unraveled

suddenly,
and so tenderly,
rekindle lost love
with one another

the tendrils of their
proper order
my mind
and it's logic

incapable of
deciphering
these disjointed
meanings

(certain nuances
I'm only now
fully appreciating)

no longer shall I be
walking the halls
of this stygian,
willful mansion
at nighttime hours

like a frightened
chambermaid
praying she's seen
to everything
before her master
wakes up

what would've been
left of my heart
upon awakening

having been
capable of

fully forgetting
all of the things
that matter?

(I know that Poe
would never
have stolen from me)

I receive a message
directed intently
at me
from beyond
his decades-old
grave

the piercing
ambiguity,
the taxing and
total lack
of any true romance

only the sour taste
of death
on the back of
my papery,
withering tongue

until I feel my voice
escaping

lead my thoughts
to wandering

his message
reinterpreting itself
unto me

then I see
so many more
staircases to
explore

his aphotic feelings
flush outwards
through the corridors
like the
navy-colored blood
in every one
of my icy veins

My Energy is Safe

with me

my soul is my own

my peace is impermeable

I radiate light from within

I am aligned with the will of the universe

my joy is a thread woven through the lines of time

my spirit is steady

unshakable as ancient mountains

I breathe deep the force of life

I allow it to create space and bounce inside my lungs

I recycle all of the energy I receive

and give it back to

thee...

Lady Luna Plays a Game

the moon is
so intrusive in the corner
of my eye

as I drive by this midnight pasture
half alive

just try to close your eye upon her
her brilliant face
is like a fatal trick

her heavy-laden impressions
weigh down
reality's bending fabric

I feel thirsty
and drawn
to her sallow complexion

I yearn to be her audience
captive and incomplete

having never
ventured to taste her
milky sweetness

my maiden, perforce haul me
inside your fragile gravity
so I can see

the thin sparks of fire
hovering just above the lack of air
in your graveyard atmosphere

they're waiting
to be ignited by footsteps
that tarry no longer

I lean back
interlocked with your
romantic power

caught in the florid waves
of the sunny side
of your face

and my soul
bows down to thee

Night on Bald Mountain

the heavy shadow
of evil itself
moves beyond itself

casting its black blanket
over all of the villages
of the world

        all at once

directionless skeletal horses
   clamber atop pathless winds

throughout the smoky horizon
   tiptoeing across midnight

they gallop through the hours
   coming and going

        leaving you

            . . .for dead

        behind in a blind,
extinguished place

        a space in which
you could never hope

           . . .to breathe

(or conceive of the thought
   of breath itself)

the latent life you've
stumbled into discarding
of your own free will

no one has anything to say
to you here
nor any comfort to give

the solitary bell
   is tolling

and you can't escape
   its thrumming beat

though you might try
   and hopelessly

           sew closed your ears

though now they're

made up of your fears

Red

the color of

        blood, lips and roses

        (chosen)

like my dead, stagnant heart

        suspended in my chest

once your

        cool blue veins

        ferry your cruelty

across highway lanes

        mellifluous longing,

        your tenderness,

backpedalled across

        distant stars, forever,

        and heading deeper

into the past

        the further

        its light travels

I've become transparent

        in your gaze,

        unnamed,

my heart snuffed out

        like a lowered

        lantern flame

Gloating in Hell

evil is often gleeful

grinning its polished teeth
    whilst gnawing your neck to ribbons

habitually getting away with murder

sleeping behind red waterfalls

on sheer-drop cliffsides

wailing from the bottom
    entreating you to remind it of its name

turn a blind ear, pretend you can't hear

for your immortal soul depends on it

my ear closes itself off,
    and seals in the extent of my thoughts

we light a fire in the cavern of my eardrum

and keep warm while the world burns outside

unrealizing that a cocksure attitude
    will be smited by time

Death's Bludgeon
(a tango)

death hovers
>death leaves no footprints
>death floats through

the decaying corridors
>of the dilapidated
>mansion in your mind

you cannot speak to death
>unless you wish
>to join him

you cannot look death
>in the eyes
>you can only steal

glances at death
>and pray with
>all of your might
>that you make it out alive

if death is in your house
>you know it immediately

the hairs on your arms
>stick up

>(best to ignore it)

>carry on
>carry on...

>WAKE UP IT'S NOT SAFE!
>DEATH IS IN THIS PLACE!

you CANNOT sit
>at his table
>without throwing all
>caution to the wind

>FOOL!
>KEEP YOUR MOUTH SHUT!
>SAY NOTHING!

why are we even
>sitting here?
>I don't remember him
>sitting down

at our table
>whose choice was this?
>who would be so

careless?

I can hear

him thinking
at me
in my own mind

he's asking me all

of the questions
I don't know the answers to

as if

coaxing me
coaxing me

I pirouette

away from him with a
swift elegance

I know the steps

to his dance

(and my footwork
is fancier)

I dominate

death's
dance floor

(this time)

Abuse
(a maze with no center)
2013

makes me

      creatively

SUFFOCATED

   no, REALLY

I can feel the

      cement walls
      closing in
      on all that's

vibrant within

the dome

of my consciousness

      STIFLED

I sniffle and

sniffle

living vicariously

      inside

      THE DANGER ZONE

(so much anger to

      be found here)

Static Sheets

when I was with
men, sexually...

when I was younger,
in my 20s...

sometimes I knew
point blank

that the thing they
were most attracted
to about me

was my trauma/
suffered abuses...

my pain
my torment

my shuddering flesh
pressed into theirs

the innocent fear
behind my eyes

they got off on
its untainted nature

its proud, nuclear core

my authentic bow
to their will...

it's like they could
sense my body

whispering,

"you are man

i am woman

and you are stronger

i fold beneath you

i succumb"

my father shut me up
with his finger

and put these words

in my mouth

to speak to all the other
men I might meet

how much did he know
back then

about the streaks
my nails left
on the walls

and on the floors

as you were dragging me
down the hallway

by my hair

to a place:

I don't know where...?

Ricocheted Love

each day is duly delicate, our lips are
locked together

your arms are wrapped around my heart, and
your words are like kisses from a distance.

I feel like you're here when you're not

I keep sensing your presence and looking
over my shoulder to check if you're there
(stalker, watch me)

only you're not anymore
and I find myself needing you to know

that you're the person I've been looking for
my entire life, and I'll be your forever girl
(fibber lies to herself)

I know you like I know myself,
maybe even better

I see you, to me your soul is see-through
(beliefs like ungranted wishes)

and lover, I love all of you
(shards of ignorance)

every inch, every nook and crevice

to me, you are a work of art
(a question of taste)

also, I can see your pain, and the other
person you once were in a past life before me
(red flags flung clearly)

I see your life as one big, beautiful
tapestry, being woven meticulously and
with care

an intricate process that led you to me
with perfect timing
(one might say too perfect)

our synchrony is the stuff of old,
timeless fables
(like the ones about witches eating kids)

they promised when I was young that
stories end with "Happily Ever After"

I wasn't sure before if it was true,
but now there's me and there's you
(he swallowed me up alive, too)

Green & Red Windowpane

I cannot understand
why all this green
outside the window
isn't affecting me
the way it did
last year
only one year ago
prancing I was
through the forest
like Donner and
Blitzen

I rushed from
then
tripped through
now
and froze my bones
during a winter
that seemed
to me
an ice age long

Why does this green
not strike me?
I knock three times
and get no answer
the vibrancy is muted
by my oh-so-stoic
ear canals

someone misplaced
the sun
and yet I'm blinded by
a whiteness
the absence of nature's
ever ever green
I don't belong stuck
in these tunnels
so stiflingly
clean

The leaves weep
with dripping rain
that slides
down the slippery
sheath of their
gray surfaces
and collects
all summer long
in tiny pools
meant solely for
the swimming of
gigantic bugs

But once the fog
creeps across the
windowpane
the curtains of
my eyelids draw back

I'll be careful
this time
not to over-blink
these eyes
lest I
forget to
keep my sight
surrendered and
color

Myth of the twisted tree trunk

there's nowhere
I'd rather be
than beside the you
of three years past

      your arm

reaching out to grasp
my waist
like there was no one
or nothing else in sight
for you

      but me

and alas, that's not you
or me anymore
unlucky for you
I'm the one whose memory
keeps the most

      accurate score

the good, the bad
and the ugly
once danced within

      our souls

a jaunty medley
rendering us incapable
of being

      happy

and now, all that's left
of our once
flourishing and

      budding love

is a decaying
intertwined tree

      trunk

the wind still blows
through our barren branches
so I can sing to you
and you to me

      and when we
      crumble

to the ground
no trace will
be left of
what once was

"we"

seedlings may make
their homes
in the lush
dirt leftovers
we lovingly

bequeathed

to lovers
caught in webs
of upcoming

calamity

you see, our death
was no failure
(not in the eyes of
newborns yet

to breathe)

take faith in the hearts of
young lovers' glee
throughout the vast cycle
of an innocent

eternity

new love will again
take root
and poke out of the ground
as a brand new

twisted-trunk tree

Clove
2013

so I said to myself:

>"by the time I finish
>smoking this clove cigarette,
>I'll know what to write"

all I know is
that I was mentally

>leaping with the
>thought that I

could write
10,000 poems

>right now if I
>wanted to

because that's what
we poets do:

>procrastinate on
>vital thoughts

meant to be
painstakingly
taken down

>only WE have the
>power to expose them

for what they are
in fullest nudity,

>coverless & pale

bodies of thought
stained with ink

>onto a page, any page

or blank space
of any kind

>(& in this day & age,
>there are so very many)

as a writer,

I find myself feverish
as I collect them,

(these blank
& empty planes)

unable to
shut myself off

once my throat
puffs with the pain

you see,
it's a little bit

like buying land,
investing in it

because you are certain

it will be worth
more later

forfeiting all
preconcieved notions

of worth, & then,
& then . . .

ambition, dedication,
above all:

self-promotion,

but in such a way
that it might benefit others

this is our true purpose,

(we human specks
on the tumultuous soils

of the Earth)

we are here
for so short a time

(considering the
expansive nature of

our planet's timeline
in and of itself),

but we're able to

regenerate ourselves
through creative output

a wise man once said:

    "you can't kill an idea,
    ideas are bulletproof"

mankind swirls along
the cosmos in an orbit

    set apart,

calm in our calamitous
certainty

    that even if we
    as a species should

die out one by one,

    (until left, there are none),

we'd still have
achieved immortality

    within the beauty
    of the cycling births

of our
bountiful thoughts

Faith in the flame

it only takes the
tiniest flame
(that is of hope)

the subconscious,
persistent tug of
undying sparks

coming from life's
most crucial and
unapologetic

       impressions of faith

a singular perfection
rotating in orbit
around our earthly home

your thoughts are
permitted to roam
where they please, simply

because an unnamed angel
will always be there
to add kindling to

the inner fireplace
that your soul keeps warm
by sending out

toasty waves of
fire-roasted compassion
throughout

       your bloodstream

making it impossible
to fall into
a kind of deepest despair

never fear, darling,
for you do not
belong there

       (I linger here for you, evermore...)

A True Artist

NEVER compromises on matters of the heart

NEVER reburies uncovered truths

my footsteps lead to the closed red curtain
and disappear on the other side of the stage

      I am become heavy drapes,

      you've left me unfurled...

and I'm creeping circles around you wearing the
black cat suit

made of

      waterfalls of velvet that trickle
into your mouth

chokes back down

      the words you meant to poison

                me with

I'll leave you and keep myself

      safely wedged between

      reality and imagination

whilst you fan the void in your eyes

      and draw veils

      across your darkness

Crypt Mining Blues

the anxiety
                is so black

it breeds only black

                my bare foot gets
stuck in it like tar

                goop sticks
between my toes

                for days and months
to follow

no one follows you
                into Amityville

(anxiety town)
                you go it alone

wearing only your bones
                (your soul is naked,

but not unpolished)
                survive the mining

                in the dark
remember all of the

                precious stone
properties

get out alive on
                a mining cart

on a track
                through the black

                you can sit
(you don't have to stand)

rest your knees
                curl them up and breathe

sigh many times
                using deep breaths to

                settle you down because
you're leaving, remember?

you bought a ticket
                to town: (one way)

not to insanity: (circular)
         you remain who you are

         as your physical properties
cannot be altered

by rust
         (unlike these ravaged rails)

Needles in my spine

there's something
  of a fortress

plunging upwards
  from the ground

in stone
  being built

upon my back
  it's filled with

dank hallways and
  echoes of silence

it's a conundrum
  being boxed up

growing an energy
  field that must

by all means
  be contained

this landscape is
  heavy to carry

around
  and every time

my spine has spasms
  I wish away

the hulking mass
  that is my past

wishing I had
  the power to

seal it up
  in a time-locked

bubble
  where nobody

can enter or exit
  for the whole

of many
  eternities

Do I haunt you like you haunt me?

together, do we skate this line

of eternity?

...from you, will I ever be free?

I know not why we dot this charred,

blackened landscape

where nothing can grow

and the birds don't sing

I can feel you pulling back the air

from my throat

greedily robbing my breath

down your own fatal lungs

it's black, too, in there...

I've escapaded around your

secret tunnels before

and I know what's curled up by

the fire inside your eyes

you cannot escape my knowing you...

you cannot hide what you've already

shown

don all of the robes you've tried on

before

I see you coming

and I'll watch you go

neverending nightmares

leave themselves like breadcrumbs

across the scattered timeline

of my knowing

of you

your demon soul

breathes in and out

just to split my hairs

in two

Embowered in the Hollow

it is enough for me
to close my eyes and see the stars

the crescendoing sound
of leaves whipped up in a breeze

I crouch in the hollow of an
old oak

undergoing a melodious and slow
decay into night

      I vanish into the breathing silence
      bewitching the lids of my eyes

      so they won't open

      upon your rustling step
      into this shady abode

you drank up the midnight
and crept along the forest floor

to where I lay amidst the vines,
like my arms I'll wrap

round and round your so tempting torso
bathed in milk-brewed moonlight

      the wandering moon crosses the sky
      and blesses the land

      where we sleep

      blue-light subtle kisses
      reflecting off of blades of grass

      and lily pads

your warmth
keeps away the chill of fog

and my heart scoops out love
in cups

poured forth into your heaving
breathless dawn

The Crystal Ship

       unforeseen stretches

       of self-forgiveness

permeating the soft outer-membrane

of the iridescent shell I made my home in

ocean waves rolling languidly overhead

       undulating whispers

       and plaintiff rhythms

hydrate my wistful thoughts of unremembering

       I drink up the thirst I find

       on this once barren plane

grateful for the tiny bits of teeming life

poking their way up

       through carpets of floating sand

A Mother is There

I had a conversation
with Mother Theresa
she was telling me
about all the tears
she'd already been
shedding for me

I felt guilty
and dried her sad eyes
with a small piece
of white silk

she looked so beautiful...

her essence comprised
of an entire world's pain
you could see it
inside the wrinkles
of her face
the folding of her hands

she gave me advice
like any good
grandmother would
and told me a story about
her own life in childhood

I'd gladly pass it along
to you, only I won't
because you've already
heard her words
deep in your own heart

and you should know
that she and I both
eternally patient,
watch over your soul

First crawl out the shell

her voice

        reaching out
   into the tunnel

but it is forbidden

        here

she's not

        noticing the
   warning signs

for only

        a moment
   she has forgotten

        the proper respect

for her
   surroundings

        the tunnel

is liquid dark

        the puddles

are deep enough
   to drown in

   but can she

        sidestep unreality

once she's already

   fallen into

   the event horizon

        of

self-deception?

Sink down

one level

to relax the brain

          having formerly perceived

     the highest plane

hang down low

in the below

       relax the tightness

    protruding the muscles

           of your mind

drift on the back

        of your consciousness

   as if floating

on a calm river

unfocus the stormy eye

of each thought

blur the line

between reality

and what it perceives

hang down

in the outermost layer

of the subconscious

massage your body here

enjoy the perfumed air...

isn't it crisp

on the tongue?

proclaim yourself

Lord or Lady

of   this   infinite   space!

allow your thoughts

to smolder

in the ebony fires

of their

former hiding

places...

entertain hypotheticals

scandalous thought experiments

shameless "what if?" scenarios

why not play out

your deepest

fantasies?

...you know

the ones you were

always the most thirsty for

but were too ashamed

to quench with the

slightest bit of water

even within the

confines of your

own bodi-mind

hear now, the rhythm

beckoning behind

the gates of

your awareness

it's a tribal place

back here

can you hear those humming

drums?

don't you want someone

to come over there

and strum

until you

come...?

What is the echo

inside your reflection?

have you used it to tame me?

with these fresh eyes

I unbelieve

knock knock

at the castle door

welcome downwards,

the gates that fall...

are we walking through tides?

or the shifting movements of time?

I sit on the broken puzzle

outside your door

and chess pieces bounce

between my knees

where are you going?

do you know where you've been?

The usefulness of my darkness

has not expired...

       hopeless romantic, drawn

to the blood

       inside the walls

       of a weeping vortex

          spiral down...

have faith

       that a trail of breadcrumbs

will illumine

          at your command

sail the neon walls

          of this twisted space

       the funneling tornado

takes you straight down

          (she...chose...down!)

       to the sparkling oubliette

cowering in waiting

does she hear the cackles

　　of the old witch who

knows her...?

　　　knows her favorite old

　moldy book?

　　　the teddy bear with its

insides freshly ripped?

　　the laughter of my name is

　　　carved along the walls

of a cave lost to time

　　　we meet here to plot

　and plunder

and pluck our breath away

　　until it withers

like the petals

　off a brown flower

　　not watered for days

　upon days...

I beseech you:

meet me here

meet me here

when the moon is new

and the spells we cast

will dance among stars

written along the lines

of obscure constellations

I'll bubble over with you

and drink the foam

back in

through my ears

I hear nothing

in this place

besides the heavy

drumming of my own

bloodthirsty heart

Passionate Whispers

our hungry tongues --

        lassoing,

predatory snakes

      we've thrown darts,
      intertwined our bodies

continuous,
      inseparable

      orgasmic thrusts

          upended and
          unprotected

mutually owning

      a new tunnel

      --connected--

          a seamless wormhole

in space

      THAT WE CREATE

as our deepest passions

          now ably overtake

      ...THE LINE

of crippling TIME,

        (so sudden)

seconds passing by

           at the behest

of a mesmerizing
rhyme

as if in a dance,

we lead our

ravenous,
interlaced limbs

through quivering,

unquenchable,

WHIMS OF A POWER

dalliance,

belonging solely

to an ancient crumbling
tower...

there's a MAD ECSTACY

blowing across rivers...

rippling in the wind/
an eternal haste

this lust-laden bubble

(that suffocates us
sometime long after
our subconscious

kicked in)

--IMPERVIOUS TO ALL THREATS--

(yet about to burst)

we tease the notions

of laws
and accepted boundaries

each of these,

dethroned with

EASE...

with not much more
than a blink and a

WINK,

our excitable bodies

now sweating out

heavy bolts...

seeping into chasms/

fever drawn claws/
your
nakedest essence/

a soul's magnetic
thrusts...

exposed and
vulnerable

triumphant JOY

our unbridled, CARNAL

jaws

that DESTROY

conceived in the soppiest

of passions,

(a vulnerability

transposed)

discarded,

    rusty shackles,

        the awe of heavenly

sweet ambrosia

    mixed with the scent

    of a warm,
    crisping bliss

soaking and

        massaging

our dehydrated

    and closing

        pores...

(they are wide open now,

    widest even as a
    baby's

FIRST GLIMPSE

    with

        DAYBORN EYES)

is there a true
and proven reality?

is it one of malleable
creation?

is it limitless in
mirrored reflections?

two imperfect dreamers

breathlessly discovering

the pathway of endless

cyclic time

...and how easily

the walls

around the unnecessary

become entirely

--PULVERIZED--

chiseling away

at the

integrity of eternity...

(like a toothpick
for the mind)

together we find

tattered,

obsolete veils

having fallen into

        piles of dust...

     (at the
very core
of the universe

you will find

      our TRUST)

Black Curtains
(the neon light of grief seeps)

Hear the piercing sound of nails in
blenders

A room spinning out of control

I'm insane and this madness uncontained
harzards a guess upon you

And reckons with your brain

The disdain of day to day life

And plucking yourself from bed, a concept
inane

Take toasts on the spinning heads of
squirrels

Drop your eyeballs into a pocket of the sun
and leave them out to rot for as many
days as it takes for them to disintegrate

I'll leave you alone in the corner at death's
doorstep

Inside you'll find the waiting room where
we chew the walls

As the clock clinging to the wallpaper confuses
the spinning of its three needles

Time and time and time again I told you to
pay attention and quit zoning out

But there's no telling you anything

You're stuck here forever

(And the polluted air muffles your shout)

I'm walking a tightrope of mind

am I my own keeper?

will my ancestors

eventually sing my

soul to sleep?

I find myself wondering

about these broken gates...

and whether or not

there's enough material left

to refasten them

no pretty bow will do

when decorating the banks

of indecorum

I'm fastidious in checking

both sides of the track

where chunks of my heart

left stains of indecision

I will not be robotic

in the gliding dance

I do to

surround you

once I'm emptied

of truth

how delicious you are...

my plump, juice-laden

forbidden

fruit

A thing or two I've learned

ABOUT GUILT:

once upon a time,

       I intentionally flicked off
my morality switch,

          shot my conscience
into space

          to suffocate

I'd been in the throes
       of my worst addictions...

          it's a terrifying moment

when the realization arrives
       that not only do you not

          respect yourself,

       but that you've actually

learned to HATE yourself
          to loathe and detest,

which in turn plants
       the deadly dangerous

          deathwish seed
down deep and firm

into the embedded soils

of your heart and mind

you can never TRULY be blind

to the deeds you do

that you know deep down

are ethically, morally

and incontrovertibly

WRONG

thank God I have found

my goddess, Gaia,

I have repented, and so my soul

has finally been reminded

how to sing

I would wring my hands forever

into the depths

of a bottomless well

only I can't keep up

such an effort

I've learned the hard way

that the one and only way

to feel guilty forever

is to NEVER forgive myself

and FORCE myself to die

I know better now

than to so readily

accept this ancient enemy,

but even so,

I'm an addict with a

faulty memory

Gaia, please let these

grateful pages

maintain my telemetry

Dearest Blue Supermoon
(a prayer)

please, part these clouds
                    turned to rough seas

that I may behold you, lovely,

                    in your full and spectacular beauty,
          mightly,

and haphazardly adorned,
                    Queen of nighttime realms

          open your arms wide,

                    reach out your pale beaming
          fingertips,

firmly clasp
          my outstretched limbs

          I hear your whispers in my heart

          I feel you penetrating my womb...

          please allow my eyes, this night,
to belong to you...

                    I pray thee, open thy navy blue
          curtain

draped heavily across
                    so many mismatched currents of air
for truly,

          the next time you lift your veil

it'll be 2037,

...and I'll no longer be
a young woman of 37

Divinity

the breath mimics

the life force of the

universe itself

we can use it to help

tether us

directly

to inexhaustible energies

breathe deep

and become

DIVINE

Lasso the breath

one must lasso the breath

        like a lonesome cowboy

dirt-grimed and standing

                on the sands

of a deserted arid plane

languidly

        mulling over the myriad violets

and umbers of the sunset

                as it creeps ever downward,

(telling no one its secrets)

colors that define

          the flow of evening light

a sight for the eyes to take in

            with little lungs

packed deeply within

                each iris

until then,

          you never realized how

all of the various

parts of your body

come to breathe

IN UNISON

had no trouble

once the vents were

THRUST OPEN!

--TAME THE WILD AIR, DRAW IT IN--

with every single one

of your lusty pores!

like smoke escaping burnt incense,
only backwards...

floating, then spiraling

towards an open window,
air dancing through canals,

bearing ALL

the stuff of life:

LASSO IT HERE!!!

train the mind and the body

to release it

where it's needed most

and more importantly,

--WHEN--

your breath will never betray you

once you have befriended

it thoroughly

into the very core

of who you are

an enduring companion

leading you along peaceful paths

where your own two feet

deserve to

and DO BELONG

Identity is my direction

I always save a piece of myself

          for myself

     even these currents of wind

know which way they're going

          we churn the air like butter

with the listed dreams

            we've let loose

     finding their way

        to the sea and back again

I believe in the protected heart

        the hapless thought

     and the intertwining

        of fractal planes

I ensconce the night

     in between my eyes

        in time for dawn each day

A prayer

Gaia continue, please...

to grow my branches
further and further outwards
into the arms of yours
so that we may intertwine
eclipsing, then recycling

        soul & mind

until our earthy matter
steps into the traces
& creeps inside
the pieces of cosmos

        unshielded by time

discarded by each dimension
(until now)
let us orbit the hips

        of collected dreams

(I never understood
  how important balance
  could be,
  until I lassoed it for
  myself to see...)

up close
& revel in the deep peace
that dwells traquilly inside
the heart & soul of harmony's

        clanging bells

juicy sweet fruit trees
transferring energies
apples repeatedly

        conking heads

ideas made of
sooty boots
trampling right on out
of a thick & shadowy

        ether

leaving footprints
for our spirits
to find their way back
to the crystalline healing

of ebbing
                pond waters

but
how many brave eyes
will humanity be willing
to heave-ho open,

                to pry?

I see the heart
of the tree
beneath damp

                brown bark

moist bedrooms
of evergreen moss
below a canopy of

                pine trees

it is they who encapsulate
the nuances of peace
rustling leaves
set on
                repeat:

TO SEE IS TO LIVE THE VIBRANCE

TO SING IS TO BE FREE

a spirit cranked open
creates
butterfly-winged
oceans

                spreading from

You

                to
Me

A sense of

spiraling through

    weighted time

and seas of stars

    so densely packed

pick-axed and stacked

    into icy walls

chipping away at eons

    time passing along

with no notice

    for the work, the purpose

carries the soul over

    each hurdle and line

drawn by the sands

    of crumbling planets

their infinite pieces

    recline in dusty spaces

lacking in air, yet

    teeming with life

undenying the persistence,

    the relentlessness

a form unfolds you've surely

    never seen before

it's vexing, and waits

    for your eyes

to change their minds

    and see the stars

for what they are

    the broken up bits

of throes of

    relinquished souls

now romping their way

    across heaven's own

Grand History

Open Doors

if a door is open

should it necessarily be walked through?

does it matter where it leads?

I close my eyes and float through hallways

in a curious ghost body

filled

with hundreds and hundreds of doors

not all of them are open,

but the ones that are

I feel

are beckoning, beckoning...

absurd answers lie therein,

but is it essential that I discover them?

don't these tales foretell themselves?

is what I'm truly seeking simply

an excuse to venture this direction?

have I tripped over my conscience

in order to tell myself

I accidentally fell into...

an asserted beginning?

rippling echoes of laughter

bounce through

my brain's

vain downtown

lanes

I'm drowning in this twilight

field

moonlight cascades across

beaming grass glades

and I'm stumbling from unreality

back again upstream

towards the dreams

I've made real

I drop

the weight of truth

like a monolith stone

on your mind

inexpression

is the dug mine

where you now live

uncomprehend all things

my lips curl

over your thoughts

sealing them tightly

within my grin

Basking on a Squeaky Line

one must be poised
             to understand...

                        (the writing can only make
          sense in this way)

whose third eye clamped shut

        when called upon to diversify?

unfed visions will starve,
                the very best ideas

             will go hungry!

shifted seats imprinted upon
                 theoretical planes...

          lines of text
                 actualizing along

             the brain's veiny membranes

like grasping at
                 rumpled gray smoke

          that chokes the throat
          as it rises upwards

I've since cored the thoughts

          that once escaped me...

                 hung them to dry
                 on my squeaky clothesline

          (she strung it up long before
          I came here,
          the woman who lived here long ago)

it's a trick of light
                 in afternoon hours

the rays of the sun come
to blind me through the window

at 2 or 3pm each day...

the days that came after
I decided to close

so many books, (the ones with

all the most useful
information)

how could I have justified
so much trust in these

rust-ridden fingers
as they'd been delicately

sewing all the pages shut?

by what needle do I
re-thread the red lines

of my eyes?

gulping down vivid sacs
of rains that never cease...

opening each of my orifices
like windows flung wide

at the first scent of Spring

I'm devouring all of the seeds
as they fall from the trees

I grasp at the knowing,
I linger at the accepting...

I challenge the vault of my mind,

(send out my raw nerves
to hang on the faulty clothesline)

My Mind

and my thoughts are an endless script

I trip upon my own scurrying fingers

                applying ink to page

    never quickly enough

I sink below each scribbled line

                dipping my toes

    down and past

                decisive paragraphs

I've melted my conundrums

down into carefully sculpted sentences

                that give form

    to my history

remembrance is paramount and tacked

with mixed up letters

                like recipes

    completed across

                the span of a lifetime

then tossed and scattered into the air

I give into the prayer that is myself

                to the forces of life

    drawn in and out

                of my chest with each breath

I turn up my palms to the sun, and let it

shine in through the gaps between my teeth

       filling my mouth deep

    and lending energy to my voice

      bubbling ever upwards

from my gut

far down below

A power unto itself

(the universe puts my father's power
in perspective,

and yet,
the Earth has one moon,
but two sexes)

there was a tangible
unseen love grasped by the
astronauts on the moon

a genuinely felt sense
beaming from us on Earth - to them

from the moon's
gaspless atmosphere
and back

(a tether that was razor thin,
and somehow comfortable)

"The moon is here, the earth is there.
I'm on the moon, this is real."

one of them had a dream
while he was there...

that he had been to the moon before...

remembered being there

with his fellow astronaut
and saw the two of them roving the
surface like doubles

theories of time and repetition of concept
breaking down the barriers

of the conscious mind
of consciousness in continuity

his subconscious had a true, deep sense of
his point in spacetime:

he HAD been there before
he will ALWAYS be there

this is his UNIQUE POINT
that NO ONE ELSE can occupy

a tangible, spiritual presence

accompanied their mission...

(3 astronauts locked in undeniability)

"I felt like I belonged.
I didn't feel like an alien on the moon.
Humans must explore.

May all mankind feel the spirit of peace
in which we came in their hearts."

the moon seems stark and uninviting
at first, foreboding

but that's because the moon reflects
cause and effect so sharply,
and with precious little nuance

past and present/chunks of rock
banging out species and history

they have no ability to
comprehend

gravity at its simplest:

a tango of huge masses: earth and moon

forever linked
by dispassionate reason

and yet they endure for all of our
philosophical ambitions

the earth has one moon, and
this is manageable
for the human mind to conceive of

our sturdy companion beams
its white light/midnight reassurances
to remind us necessarily of sun

it sets a rhythm for the wombs of women
in time with waves and tides

cresting motions that
mimic a woman's hip,
the waters fall and rise:

the moon is with us when the men are not,

but only men have actually set foot there...

Unburying Treasures

it is through my own words

       that I know myself

untinged by time

and dilapidation

I extend my consciousness out

       to the whirlpools of heaven

driven back by understanding

terse remembering

I break apart into myself

       and dip my toes

       into the spreaded cream

of forever

only to find, that again

I am who I say I am

       and who I will be

half-flung truths

       creep-crawl away from me

       on tired twigged limbs

limping forwards

       towards the golden paths

of a mirage

reflections in pools

     long since dried up

having been drunk down

by the many fools

     who unfolded their voiceboxes

     and set them out to sizzle

in unrelenting sunbeams

I weave time backwards

     and down upon itself

creating layers of reality

that even my own pride cannot deny

sucking silken threads

     between my teeth

clearing the way for further humble prayers

my heart's absolution is revealed

only after the false mirrors

     have reflected enough light

     to burn my last few cadences

     at the stake

     and by now

my spirit comes to know itself

     and swims in sychrony

with the tale

the universe wrote about me

upon its very back

I reckon with this vibrance

an unknown,
strange kind of peace
hammering its way through the air
and across my brow

the blue strips of lake tucked between
the hills in the valley below
are like crescent smiles

reaching out to reassure
the exhausted limbs
of my hiker's humble body

far-reaching tranquility
stretches across my nimble psyche
and I feel as though
I'm born again

(a fever soothed,
uncertainty recoiled)

my dreams paintbrush themselves
onto the very top
of this sun-drenched, airblown
mountain summit

and I can taste the delicious
peacefulness of this place
on every corner of my hungry tongue

This is the fix

you keep trying

                                        to direct it

try unfocusing your mind

                instead

         remember: EXPANSE

                           vast wide landscapes

for wanderers to

                  roam in

don't tiptoe any longer

                  or else your
                  voice may get stuck

in a MONO-

             TONE

            (which is

                  good for nothing,

other than stoning
peoples' ears)

                      (I can feel mine
                growing tired)

having UNfocused

my mind's
        thoughts

                they now detach
                themselves

    from the bars

of their prior
        prison cells

indicating it's

                  time

for the release

        of sheer
        immaterial

            translucent silk

that only a morning's dawn

        might weave
          before bed

FEEL
        THIS   CAPRICE!

        outward dashing
          of lighted dots

    trotting
        across my mind

the swirling
        gathering
                tethering

of life

and information

unfocus: NOT!

              FOCUS!

    live within
the everything

My Pixie

        muse, you're a

Water Dancer...

        my answer to
layered depths

        of self-denial

        your wings

 are fused onto
        the backs

of floating
        bits of oxygen

I breathe you in
        while you

tranquilize

        my insight
in the most

        perverse of ways

I'm trespassing
        on the hinges

of your
        concentration,

and like a thief
        in the night,

        I steal all of
your attention

        for myself

        before we fall
into the bed

I tiptoe in
        barefeet

        all around
        the room

lighting candles until

we writhe...

(as though
        under a spell)

I smile into
        your ear

        where you can't
see me

and whisper

all sorts of things

too quietly
        for you to hear

my mind has become
        fluffy clouds

        to tumble in,

but I find
        myself

        pushing and pulling

instead

My eyes

glued on Jupiter on the ride home

> missed most of the sunset

> mountain nooks now shadowing the light

Jupiter is close by...

> her point in the sky mesmerizing my sight

> and my thighs are quaking...

she raises her noxious shield

> and swings her wide, maternal hips

> bouncing away the hurtling asteroidal rocks

(gargantuan death headed straight for us)

> I see her so clearly in this navy sky...

is she calling to me?

is she asking me to witness her?

> I am searching for the hidden seams

> through which we may speak

she asks me to send her

> cloud-formed etchings of my soul

> (she's already met me halfway)

I'll kiss her hands and bow

> my head in gratitude

> for the mercy of her stance in our sky

(truly, Jupiter was never a king, never just some guy)

Jupiter is an Earth mother

        who has protected us all our lives

        throughout space and time

she has become our very sense of the Divine

I mark myself as her daughter

        happily allowing her churning winds

        to guide my spirit through life's

great seasons

Then the light

turned to yellow
on the evening when we ventured out
into the storming rain...

a heavy golden drape
sank into the very air
a nebulous cloud
of amber light sat heavy

these were hues we got folded into
by the likes of sticky sap
evaporating out of old maple trees

before I'm crystallized
into this moment forever
I see you driving us forwards and through
these sun-soaked highways

hovering beyond the gravitation
of tired reality

I draw you to me after the road bends
and kiss your honey-tinted mouth
so deep

we'll swim and
never come up again
for the salty sweetness
of this ochre air

Entwine

        like the tendrils of roots
growing into the

        cranial spaces of my brain

I accept the nurturing spread

        it leaves a trail of
strengthened vision

        all the way to the maze's end
the teeth of the

        twisted snake pattern

poke little holes
        just underneath my skull

        once they penetrate
the spongy tissue layers

        hooks spring out and fasten

themselves together
        cradling my psyche and my soul

What is this Earth?

with immortal
rolling hips

       that dip and stretch on
       towards infinity?

I sit near the gnarled
and twisted tree

       she grabs onto the cliff's edge
       desperately as teeth clenched tight

and winds and weaves
eons of wisdom

       throughout her trunk
       and leaves...

throttle my soul
tumble straight down this sheer hill

       spending so much time
       deliberately sunning the hole of my throat

air is escaping past my hair
beyond my balmy cheeks

       where I can't see it lassoed around
       those distant mountain peaks

why does it feel like I've been here before?
to this strange and thriving summited throne?

       I do not look down on this view
       instead, I exchange it in my mind

for a memory
or two

Sunset on the highway

hills the color of honey...

        gazing down a blinding
   stream of sun

eyesight torn and wrapped

        in tufts of fading light

she's settling down

        and over and

   down

I trace her steps apace

        high time I close my eyes
        witness to

               grace...

but which deviated path
        do I take?

I've spun myself up

      in the sun's silken robes
      I uncomplicate

        the things that I see

and reach out

      to feel the colored ribbons
      that tie us together

        to form a picture

        unlocked beauty

spread it in a sheen
      like warm butter

        make certain it's coating

your lips and your eyes...

I see now that
you've been melting into me

I can feel you paddling
        inside my pores

            have I caught your gradual dripping

        into each of these holes?

now how is it

        I didn't notice this sun-drenched

            penetration before?

From how many different angles can you enjoy a day?

if you could re-live your last one

what decisions would you change?

so many split tunnels,

forks scattered for you to take

and eat your last meals

hidden away in a crevice, you try

to obscure your sense of despair

with lofty shadows, grown so vast

it becomes impossible to escape the vortex

and so you dream of the seam,

of the lip,

of the megaton black hole

you dive into spiraling bands of

of twisted light, knowing full well

you cannot escape the shrinking dawn

but you can in fact choose

the music you'll listen to

once you've pressed 'flush' on the drain

(insanity is just another word for choosy,

and doing backstrokes doesn't make you crazy)

we hear the hum of the tidal hymn

of ever-compressing matter

as it doubles over towards infinity

but never quite reaching it

I stretch myself just as long as thin

gobbling down pieces of stars

to build back strength once again

and I've deemed it a worthy endeavor

to creep back in

and out

of reality's engorged

flipbook world

www.ingramcontent.com/pod-product-compliance
Lightning Source LLC
Chambersburg PA
CBHW052114030426
42335CB00025B/2977